CREATING
HEAVEN
WHEREVER I AM

CREATING
HEAVEN
WHEREVER I AM

∞

PAIN TO PARADISE, TRAUMATIC EXPERIENCES GIVING WAY TO THE VALUES & LOVE WITHIN

JANINE NAUS

Copyright © 2017
by Janine Naus

All rights reserved, including the right to reproduce this work in any form whatsoever, without permission in writing from the publisher, except for brief passages in connection with a review.

Cover photo by Sam Schooler,
www.unsplash.com/@sam
Cover design by Rob Williams,
www.fiverr.com/cal5086

First edition

For more information please contact Janine Naus at www.janinenaus.com

ISBN 978-0-9985312-0-5

ebook ISBN 978-0-9985312-1-2

DEDICATION

I'd like to dedicate this book to my parents James and Virginia, thank you for bringing me into this world to experience, create and love. To Priscilla Dean (Mom II), thank you for loving me as your daughter and continuing to share your inspirational wisdom. To longtime friends Mavis Ranke Keyes and Bridget Zenz Evans, each of you hold a special place in my heart…I am forever grateful for you being an important part of my life. To Lisa Zalovick, who by example, inspired me to take a leap of faith in my own life. To Brad Jones, my writing muse and Chris Hackett, my creative muse. And finally, I cannot even begin to express how grateful I am to my mentor and teacher HeatherAsh Amara who came into my life exactly when I needed her. To all who touched my life as my teachers, I am grateful for the experiences we shared.

Thank you God! I am creating heaven wherever I Am. And God said, "I Am that I Am."

I AM the Tree of Life within you. My life will and must push forth, but it will do it by gradual and steady growth. You cannot come into your fruitage before you have grown to it. Remember, My life is all the time building you up into the perfection of health and strength and beauty, that must express outwardly as it is even now expressing within. You have begun to realize I AM within, but not yet learned to commune with Me, listen and learn now."

~Joseph S. Brenner, The Impersonal Life

CONTENTS

Chapter 1: Infinite Gifts of Values Within You.....1

You have a yearning in your heart, mind, and soul for love, happiness, and joy. You are aware the answer is within.

Chapter 2: Integrity 15

You ALWAYS listen to the inner voice and never lose faith of what exists in each of us. Pure integrity allows us all to forever feel whole and complete.

Chapter 3: Authenticity 21

Your 100% committed to living (and loving!) a life aligned with your values.

Chapter 4: Compassion 31

Your compassion is boundless and shines throughout, helping you to naturally understand and care for your own trauma and that of others.

Chapter 5: Truthfulness 39

To create heaven, you MUST be honest with yourself and others. Mask NO secrets and share your truth with complete compassion, limitless love, and undeniable understanding.

Chapter 6: Personal Development......................43

> Arriving at this point in your journey isn't by luck, nor is it by chance; your inquisitive and curious nature to positivity in life has got you here.

Chapter 7: Authentic Love..................................45

> You're devoted to authentic love – through compassion, patience, kindness and determination to understand everyone who needs your help, advice or simply lend your ear.

Chapter 8: Inspiration...49

> It doesn't matter who you are, or what life's thrown at you...trauma will ALWAYS pass. You inspire others to never give up hope and tirelessly reassure them that they'll find perfect harmony within themselves.

Chapter 9: Putting It All Together 55

> Be yourself. You are the creator of your own reality.

Chapter 10: Your Next Steps 59

> Define your values and set your goals.

Chapter 1: Infinite Gifts of Values Within You

You have a yearning in your heart, mind, and soul for love, happiness, and joy. You are aware the answer is within.

If you are reading this book, it is by no accident. Arriving at this point in your journey isn't by luck, nor is it by chance; your inquisitive and curious nature to positivity in life has got you here. Yes, you've experienced trauma, and you are all too familiar with continually making choices based on the expectation of others. You've realized there were times in your life where you've felt "stuck" because you were living other people's expectations, desires and values and not your own. You may have even found it difficult or even painful to break free from such choices. But today you are ready…today you've become aware that you are not living authentically and you find it is nearly impossible to stay with those choices. You've decided to begin to step beyond trauma by becoming 100% committed to living (and loving!) a life aligned with YOUR values. And now you begin to look within to deal with life changes as well as gain insight and wisdom to be your authentic self.

It's time. Your time.

Your time to leave all the sadness behind.

Let go of your feelings of powerlessness. Of hopelessness.

To open your heart and love yourself. And trust the love of others.

And know an unshakeable serenity, peace, and sense of well-being. No matter what.

Yes, I know you've already tried to make the best of it.

You've tried talking about your experience with your family and friends. But they didn't fully understand.

Perhaps you've talked with your pastor or religious leader…or gone to therapy…or read numerous self-help books.

But you still feel frustrated, disconnected and alone.

I struggled nearly my whole life with being out of touch with my feelings, putting up with abusive situations, unable to set clear boundaries and becoming overwhelmed by life, steering clear of any kind of intimate relationships, living my life in a flatlined state, never experiencing any extreme highs or lows, and a distrust of others all of which were a direct result of being physically, emotionally and sexually abused from age 3 to 50.

Like you. I tried everything.

And it wasn't until my 50th birthday when I was severely shaken after being mauled by a drunk man in a bar, that I'd reached my limit, I'd had enough. I had to get help. Real help.

Then one-day a friend posts a quote on Facebook about not taking anything personally by don Miguel Ruiz, author of the book *The Four Agreements*. I read the book, loved it, and through synchronistic events, I discovered an online radio program by one of his apprentices, HeatherAsh Amara, and author of the best-selling book *Warrior Goddess Training*. I responded to so many things she was saying, such as how to get your power back, that I signed up for her yearlong women's program. I also learned tools that helped me feel safe for the very first time...safe enough to deal with my trauma experiences, process them, and start to feel whole, powerful and divine.

As a result of my own transformation, I became certified as a life coach and expanded upon those skills with multiple trainings for one single purpose—to help YOU heal and create heaven wherever you are.

So let me ask you now…

Have you reached your limit?

Are you ready to finally get the support, guidance, and healing you need to:

- Leave all the sadness behind?
- Reclaim an open heart, love yourself again and trust the love of others?
- Have more energy, a stronger sense of self and a lot more self-confidence?
- Be free of your fears once and for all?

If so, it would be my honor to share with you the gifts I've been given through healing my own traumatic experiences so you too can be liberated from the painful emotions, frustration, and emptiness that prevents you from finding lasting joy, love, and peace.

I know what you're up against.

And I know, without a doubt, that no matter what you're feeling right now, you can heal and create your own kind of heaven wherever you are. You can be happy and healthy. You can know true love. You can live with confidence, courage, and joy.

I began with identifying my values to begin to create the life I have today. As I explored my values, I soon realized there are gifts within each value. My values guide and shape my priorities and responses to life experiences. My inspired actions and thoughts are aligned with my values…and I am experiencing a whole lot of happiness and joy. You can too!

You can create the life you want. You can create anything you desire. You can create heaven wherever you are (the "I AM")…and the 'I Am' is the healing power within you. You can create a new dream. There is no limit on your power to heal and transform every aspect of your life. You can live in harmony, truth, and love. By creating heaven wherever you are (the 'I Am') you are taking inspired actions. You affirm that you are the 'I Am' power. You are asking the power within you to open the doors to infinite possibilities life has before you. It's as if you are ushering in a breath of fresh air…breathing in the "I" and breathing out the "Am." You have awakened to the breath to reach into the deepest realities of life and to reach your highest states of consciousness. It is your path to your essence, your core, your soul, your heart. It is the source energy within you, and it is experienced through a profound feeling in your heart…it is your great wisdom within. You accept the great mystery that you are an individuation of God, Goddess, Spirit, Universe (whatever higher power or supreme being you align yourself to). You are the "I Am that I Am" as written in so many religious and spiritual texts. You are consciousness. Because of your awareness, you are the creator of the heaven you choose to live in life, no matter where you are in life.

You walk your unique path in life. The same is true for your breath…no one can breathe for you. Yet as you breathe, you realize we all breathe the same breath. Your breath contains the same molecules and atoms of every being for all of time. Yes, you are breathing my breath as I am breathing yours. Your breath in me becomes the breath of every species on Mother Earth tomorrow. You are breathing your ancestors' breath as I am breathing theirs. You are breathing for all of life because without breath, there would be no life. Your breath came from the same source of all of life.

The same can be said about your beliefs, your points of view. Your beliefs can impact your experience with breath. If your beliefs are negative, your breath becomes constricted. If your beliefs are positive, your breath deepens and expands within your body. There is a wealth of wisdom in our breath…the space between our in and out breaths. It helps you to look at things with clarity and put them in perspective. Sink into what is important to you. What do you value most? What is most important to you in life? Your values guide and shape your priorities and responses to life experiences. Your inspired actions and thoughts are aligned with your values. Focusing on your breath keeps you out of your mind so you can follow your heart free of all the chatter in your mind.

To create heaven wherever you are (the 'I Am') starts with you. When you see who you really are and shift your beliefs to your highest good, you can create heaven wherever you are in life. And when you create heaven wherever I Am, you also create heaven for all of humanity.

Why is it that you have such a yearning in your heart, mind, and soul for love, happiness, and joy? You are not alone as we all do. What do you need to do to fulfill that yearning…others seem to have done it. Simply ask about what your purpose is in life and who you are. Ask youself, "What is my purpose in life? Who am I?" "What do I value most in life?" A response often leads to determining your core set of values. Your core values are the pillars to what you want and a bridge to your purpose in life. Your values help you manifest all that you want in your life. There are an infinite number of core values, and they all already exist within you.

In this book, 'I Am' sharing seven of the infinite number of values available to you along with how you can bring the gifts of these values in your life. All values are already within you. The 'I Am' in you means you are the giver and the gift. The 'I Am' is the gift to you. There is no work necessary as your divine voice will help you make the wise choice of values that are aligned with your true purpose.

Your values are the quality of your core and who you are as source energy in a receiving mode. You choose and define values that resonate at a vibrational frequency with your core. Your values stem from the energy of love with a resonance of feeling good…things always working out is what's at the core. You recognize the Universe is based on all that is good in this moment and everything before there is a death and a re-emergence in the non-physical and leaving behind all that is not wanted. The core that re-emerges is good. And then you go through the cycle again—sifting, sorting and refining your core values—and you ask again in the next experience of death of the old to release what is no longer serving you. You recognize your core values is simply a widdling down of what is important to you in that moment. It is like a mirror reflecting back all that is good to you for your benefit and pleasure.

You have a conversation with your inner being about who you really are. When goodness in you is synched with your inner being, you are in a vibrational match. If there is not a match, meaning something feels wrong, it indicates there lies a distortion of the truth…as there is nothing really wrong. You simply find a new way of looking at things with a higher vibrational thought.

You want a core value that feels good so you can feel the connection—that which I Am. You think and feel your way through...your feeling is the evidence. When the feeling evidence of your core value is enough, then all of the other evidence must follow. Once your core values turn into a manifestation, you stay there because through awareness you see more...it is called contrast. If you stay with that core value in that moment, you are what you feel...it is what you desire. Your desire is your intention, and with intent, you have infinite possibilities to accomplish what you desire. Witness your becoming as it reflects change...your transformation. Your constant becoming feels good...a desire that you already manifested in your energy field.

Let's take a look at seven potential core values and examine how to bring the gifts of these values in your life.

1. **Integrity** – You ALWAYS listen to the inner voice and never lose faith of what exists in each of us. Pure integrity allows us all to forever feel whole and complete.

2. **Authenticity** – You're 100% committed to living (and loving!) a life aligned with your values and purpose.

3. **Compassion** – Your compassion is boundless and shines throughout, helping you to naturally understand and care for your own trauma and that of others.

4. **Truthfulness** – To create heaven, you MUST be honest with yourself and others. You mask NO secrets and share your truth with complete compassion, limitless love, and undeniable understanding.

5. **Personal development** – Arriving at this point in your journey isn't by luck, nor is it by chance; your inquisitive and curious nature to positivity in life has got you here.

6. **Authentic love** – You're devoted to authentic love–through compassion, patience, kindness and determination to understand everyone who needs your help, advice or simply to lend your ear.

7. **Inspiration** – It doesn't matter who you are, or what life's thrown at you…Trauma will ALWAYS pass. You inspire others to never give up hope and tirelessly reassure them that they'll find perfect harmony within themselves.

The Gift of Values are Always There

You are well aware that life can be painful, joyful, and somewhere in between. You are aware of the beautiful gifts life brings every day although your senses at times try to tell you differently. Why is that? The truth is, you simply lost sight of the gifts in the haze of your struggle in life. The gifts are always there. They have not left you. Be still. Be willing to be present enough to re-focus on those gifts. Every gift in life is available to you.

You have a unique set of core values that help you determine what is important to you. You may be like most people and may not know what your core values are when asked. You may be walking through life feeling like something is missing or wrong in your life, but you do not know exactly what that is. You may feel this way because you are unclear of your values and what is important to you. You simply were not aware…so be gentle with yourself as you can easily create your core values. One way to determine your values is to see how you can bring the gifts of values into your life…in reality, all values you can imagine already exist within you. Seeing the gifts of values within you can help you find the values you most resonate with. Your values can shift throughout your lifetime as the changing seasons. You honor yourself. You are true to yourself. You do the things that bring you happiness. You have faith in yourself.

So why are you not aware of your values? If you focus on external demands of life or the conditioning of your beliefs by those around you, awareness of your values become blurred lines. You can shift your awareness to what is important to you. You ask yourself, "What is it that I desire?"

You have the ability to manifest anything your heart desires. You have a power within you. You are aware of it because it is the profound feeling in your heart that you get when you reach out to what it is you desire in life. It is a force that provides you the great wisdom to achieve what you desire…and you already possess it. This power always exists even if your senses tell you differently. Dream what it is you want into being. Use your imagination…act as if it has already arrived. Whatever you desire, there is an energy behind that thought that brings into being what it is you desire. You let God know what your heart truly desires. You recognize that whatever it is you are thinking about, God gives to you—whether you are intentionally thinking of it or not. You know exactly what it is you want in life. You feel your life is overflowing with things that matter to you most. You listen to your intuition. You are perfect love. You are connected to your personal power. Your inward journey can be a powerful experience…be still, find your center for inspiration to come your way.

What you picture or imagine for a value you are wanting does not necessarily mean you will experience it until you engage your energy with the value to feel it. The power of your thoughts can be balanced or unbalanced to what it is you desire…and it is based on how you are feeling at the time. It's your emotional response to that thought…if you feel good about that value, you manifest it within your body, witnessing it, and then experience it. You draw to yourself the thoughts you need so you can experience the value you are focusing your energy on. A value is simply a thought.

You draw on the thought of your value as if it has already manifested…because it was already a thought in our collective conscious…it already exists…you are basically creating more of it by reading this book…simply being is the how of anything you want in life. Slow down and see that. Your life unfolds to your own choosing. You always maintain a Higher thought in mind as it is ever present. You stay present with this awareness. You choose this path because your beingness will help you no longer suffer. You are the image of the light you already have within.

Chapter 2: Integrity

You ALWAYS listen to the inner voice and never lose faith of what exists in each of us. Pure integrity allows us all to forever feel whole and complete.

"Faith is seeing light with your heart when all your eyes see is darkness."

~anonymous

Integrity comes from wholeness. Your heart, mind, and will are unified. You enhance your integrity by seeing the big picture…consider the whole both internally and externally. You live with integrity by discerning what your chosen values are and set out to live by them. You ask yourself, "How does what I do or fail to do affect the whole?" Once you make a decision, there is no doubt in your mind you are stepping into an inspired action. Your heart and will know without a doubt…inspired actions come from a feeling of love.

How to Bring Gifts of Integrity in Your Life?

a. **Follow Your Heart.** Follow your heart, as your inner wisdom is always there to help you make decisions that are right for you. Be in the moment…enjoy what is inside of you.

b. **You Have the Right to Authentic Safety – Journey Toward It.** You are a sacred being…just be. You create a safe container for yourself to feel all of your emotions safely. You have the ability to be with your emotions, hold them, express them to others, and have them mirrored back safely. You experience the emotions in your body and allow it to flow through your body. You choose emotions that you will or will not respond to. You have the ability to bring awareness into any emotion that arises.

How to journey to your authentic safety?

Consider using this visualization:

Settle into a comfortable position either sitting or lying down. Close your eyes, take a deep breath in and gently release it. Repeat. As you inhale, feel the support of what it is beneath you…now expand that awareness to the ground beneath that—if you are not already sitting or lying on the ground—imagine feeling Mother Earth. You are connecting deeply to her…feeling supported. As you exhale, let yourself feel the support of what supports you. Take a few moments to focus on your breathing and your physical sensations of what is supporting your body. Begin to focus on your heart…notice the physical and emotional sensations as you focus on your heart…is it full? Is it empty? Do you have a heavy heart or is it light? Does it feel separate or is it connected? Simply notice what is happening with your heart without judgement…just be with what you are experiencing.

Think of a time when you felt emotional safety…where were you? Were you with anyone? Recall your experience. Feel your feelings. Identify how you feel emotionally. How does your heart feel? Notice the sensations in your body as you think about that experience for a few moments. Simply be.

Now, think of a time when you did not feel emotional safety…where were you? Were you with anyone? Recall your experience. Feel your feelings. Identify how you feel emotionally. How does your heart feel? Notice the sensations in your body as you think about that experience for a few moments. Simply be.

Now contrast your two experiences of emotional safety. Notice the differences in your thoughts, emotions and feelings in your body. Pause. You can open your eyes and feel present here.

Move at your own comfortable pace to build trust and establish emotional safety. You have an inner knowing of your own pace to engage and relate to others. Create space for yourself by slowing down, going inside; allow for emotional and physical sensations. You take inspired actions that are in line with your heart. You are attentive to the needs of others and aware of their behavior with others. You define appropriate boundaries for yourself and others. You begin to create space for yourself to feel your experience and learn to be present with yourself.

c. **You Accept Life on Life's Terms**

Once you step into your safe space, you begin to see how you can accept life on life's terms. You begin to accept the ups and downs of life…because your newfound awareness brings choice in life. You have infinite choices available to you. Your choice impacts the experiences you may have in life. You understand the outcome of your choice may not always be known…experiences that may be in contrast to your highest good. Your free will can set the course of your choice and how you may respond to what life may present to you. You connect with your heart to bring awareness to your mind for all choices. You are empowered to choose at your heart's content…present with your goals and focused on your future. By being still and using your intuition, you dream into different scenarios of choice. Your stillness makes choice for your highest good easier as you know yourself and what you value.

When making choices, you not only think about how your choice will affect you but how it will affect others. You understand there are consequences to all of your choices. You are aware of how your choices create what you will experience. You are aware your desire to create your highest possible experience directly correlates to how you feel in the moment. You choose to fill your body with the feeling of love. By choosing to allow love to be your focus, you draw to yourself thoughts that allow you to experience such love now and in the future. You also have the ability to change your mind thus changing your thoughts, feelings, and beliefs…putting the brakes on creating a future thought experience. What you are actually doing is releasing what no longer supports that desired experience.

Chapter 3: Authenticity

You're 100% committed to living (and loving!) a life aligned with your values.

"Authenticity is embracing your vulnerability, your stillness, and owning all your superpowers. It's accepting and loving what is, not what "should be."

~HeatherAsh Amara

You are a wiser, more authentic you.

Since you are wholehearted and authentic, you embrace vulnerability. You believe that a life aligned with your values and purpose is a life committed to living and loving. Your vulnerability allows you to connect with others. You believe you are worthy of love. You belong to the greater whole.

How to Bring Gifts of Authenticity in Your Life?

Through mindfulness, you begin to pay attention to your thoughts and emotions of your current experience and observe them in a non-judgmental manner. Your attention and non-judgmental ways help you overcome any sticky point to coming to know yourself. You begin to see yourself in a desirable light. You also feel negative emotional reactivity ease as a boost of self-esteem arises in you. Through connection to your source you may see the truth about yourself. Here are some helpful tools:

a. **Ground Yourself.** You start bringing gifts of authenticity in your life by centering and grounding yourself. This simple and quick process helps you feel connected to your guides, spirits, angels, deities or who you feel aligned with so they may help you feel safe and connected to your nature, your essence—which is love.

   Here is a short grounding practice you can do…there are many ways to ground. Grounding is a helpful practice for days when you feel overwhelmed, stressed or unbalanced. When we center and ground, it helps us come back into our bodies and balance our energy. The practice helps increase personal joy and spiritual health. Grounding is easy to do and can be done anywhere. After you read this short grounding, close your eyes and think about the questions as you scan your body.

Short Grounding Practice

Close your eyes and begin to breathe in an easy, natural way. Draw your breath deeper and notice it flowing throughout your body. Slowly exhale to clear your mind and open your heart. With each breath, you are becoming more deeply relaxed.

Begin to notice how you are feeling. How do you feel emotionally? How does your body feel? Now observe the energy in your body. What does it feel like? See yourself taking in more energy with every breath. Imagine the energy flowing through you…your feet taking root to the ground below you growing deeper with each breath. Notice your breath making you feel energized and alive. When you have completed scanning your body and taken a few breaths, open your eyes and notice how you feel.

You are now ready to take the next steps that will help you begin your journey to a happy and joyous life.

b. **Breathe in Deeply; Your Breath is Precious.** You have awakened to your breath as it is the essence of you—your heart and soul. You are grateful for your breath as it makes your life possible. You also recognize your breath reminds you of the Oneness of all. You are aware the breath in you was in you before as it has been for all of life…every species that has come and gone on Mother Earth breathes the same breath. We all breathe the same breath. You breathe in the breath of all of your ancestors bringing great wisdom to your mind and body. Your breath is your prayer and is a reflection of your faith and trust. You feel the power of God within you as you inhale and His grace as you exhale. Through your breath, you express forgiveness, gratitude and surrender to all of life. Your breath aides all that may ail you—your stresses, your blocks, your fears, your pain.

c. **Develop Daily Rituals – Bring More Grace Into Your Life**

- **Set 6 Inspired Actions.** You envision what it is you desire so your thoughts and actions will be guided by inspired actions. These actions are the direct result of the Law of Attraction at work…like attracts like.

    1) **Set Your Intention for the Day, Say Thank You.** To manifest your dreams and make solutions-oriented choices in life, you choose to bring attention to what it is you desire in life along with the intention of what you want to bring to that moment.

2) **Exercise** – Move out of your head and into your body; take a walk in nature to remind you how beautiful life is.

3) **Journal** – To relax and focus on the present moment. Create a daily journal of things that make you happy.

4) **Meditate** – You meditate daily and on an ad-hoc basis as needed. You are aware of the benefits of meditating (for example, to relax, relieve stress, sleep better, ease pain, etc.).

5) **Nourishment** – You choose healthy meals and snacks...such as simple, whole and organic food that is not only healthier but pleasurable.

6) **Rest** – "Let's begin by taking a smallish nap or two."~Winnie the Pooh. You are intentional about getting enough rest to focus and create your very best.

- **Practice Gratitude – Create a Gratitude Journal.** You create a daily journal to express gratitude.

"The more you practice gratitude, the more you see how much there is to be grateful for, and your life becomes an ongoing celebration of joy and happiness."

~don Miguel Ruiz

You feel compassion, love, and understanding for others…and that brings gratitude into your heart. You are aware gratitude brings your attention into the present moment. You recognize that what you place your attention on expands in your life. As you express gratitude for all the positive experiences in life, you invite the Universe to give you more of what you want. You've got faith that gratitude helps you find more meaning and joy in life. You consistently take a few moments each day to focus on the blessings you experience each day. You cultivate gratitude to experience a deeper level of happiness, fulfillment, and well-being. You create a daily gratitude journal to express who or what inspired you, brought you happiness, and brought you peace and serenity.

- **Trust Your Intuition – Follow Your Heart.** Your intuition is the gift within you that always provides the awareness you need to choose the best direction to go in life. You are aware its answer is true for you! You understand your intuition is the energy source behind who you are and the connection to your authentic self. You follow your heart by listening to your inner voice (which may be a feeling, a nudge, or a knowing sense). You are aware of what it is that is influencing it.

  You follow your heart by slowing down and asking yourself, "What does my heart say? What do I feel? What does my spirit say?" You understand that asking these questions helps you shift from the thoughts in your head into the space where your intuition flows. You are aware that your intuitive thought is telling you something because of a spontaneous feeling arising out of it. You repeat the intuitive thought out loud so you don't forget it. When you name it, it becomes yours. You refrain from any judgment of the thought and ask if it feels true. If it is true, it will feel open and expansive…if it is not true, it is a thought from your mind.

- **Forgive Yourself and Others – It's Essential to Your Well-Being**

    Your ability to forgive yourself and others is an expression of your compassion and strength. You see others in a positive light rather than seeing their shadows within your mind. You recognize the humanity of all people.

- **Appreciate Yourself and Your Worth – You Matter**

    - **Give yourself permission to be you.** You are aware no one else is going to give you permission to be you. You are authentic and honest with yourself. You have the will to follow your passion because you know what it is you want in life. No matter the situation, you move forward one step at a time casting aside fear and any obstacles that stand in your way.

- **You are exceptional and amazing.** You feel truly exceptional. You are amazing, important, needed, unique, and confident just by being exactly who you are.

  - **Practice self-love.** You are unique, so you practice self-love in whatever way makes you feel better. One example is that you are aware your thoughts preceed your emotions and behavior…so you may practice daily affirmations. You start with the phrase "I Am" and add any statement that makes you feel good.

- **You are Loved and Needed by Others**

  - **Be vulnerable and authentic – people who value who you are need you.** You've let go of who you should be to be who you really are. Your ability to connect with others through empathy and love has drawn people toward you.

You matter, and you have a sincere belief in others... because they matter too.

- **Share your story and speak your truth.** You have a story. You experienced difficulties and may have secretly struggled with your own inner battles. Yet somehow you've overcome and survived. You speak your truth distancing yourself from your 'perceived story'. As you share your story and speak your truth you share inspiration and wisdom to those who continue to struggle. You create an emotional distance from any limiting statement in the story because you truly know who you are...you were and will always be enough.

Chapter 4: Compassion

Your compassion is boundless and shines throughout, helping you to naturally understand and care for your own trauma and that of others.

"Waking up this morning, I smile. Twenty-four brand new hours are before me. I vow to live fully in each moment and to look at all beings with eyes of compassion."

~Thich Nhat Hanh

Compassion is a gift you give yourself and others. You develop compassion by practicing it daily. You open your heart to another person. You empathize with another who is suffering. You imagine you are going through their suffering while you have equanimity in you too. You understand this to mean it is about allowing 'it' to be what 'it' is…and at the same moment you allow your heart that wants to do something about it reach out to the other person. You also reflect on how you would want your suffering to end. You reflect on how happy you would be if another person desired your suffering to end, and acted on it. You would become happy and so would the other person. You are gentle with yourself and others. You've created a loving relationship between you and the other person that is no longer based on fear.

When you feel you lack compassion, you ask yourself, "Could I have done this differently?" You stop and take a breath, step back, and look at the bigger picture so you can see the reason you are doing what it is you are doing. You realize you made a mistake as your struggle is simply part of a bigger picture you may not have been aware of. This awareness brings compassion in your life.

Your experiences in your life, perhaps since childhood, may have created struggle or caused you to harden or to try and protect yourself. Since you've experienced trauma you understand and care for your own trauma. You understand most people you meet may be struggling or secretly dealing with their own internal pain. You are aware many have gone through painful experiences that traumatized them and continue to struggle. You observe they may act in ways that are not kind as they believe this is a way to protect themselves from potential danger. When you meet anyone who struggles to overcome their own trauma you reach out to them with compassion, love and understanding. You are aware that you can look at that person from a different perspective, one of compassion, as you understand they did not consciously intend to harm anyone. You are aware it is their unconscious response to behave this way and they are unaware of the consequences of their actions.

Reflecting on your life you've begun to grasp how you may have hurt yourself or possibly someone else. Again you know you simply made a mistake. You are human and know mistakes happen.

Your bringing compassion in your life means you are open enough to learn what you would do differently next time. You are not trying to avoid the consequences of your action. Your compassion allows you to soften, be open and be present…to be in a new relationship with yourself and others.

You find compassion for yourself and others by practicing it. You ask yourself, "What does compassion feel like in my body?" When someone else struggles you explore what that compassion feels like…then bring that feeling toward yourself. You always step back to look at the bigger picture of life and replace negative thoughts with positive ones. You just simply ask how to bring compassion to yourself in that moment and make a new choice. You have a deep knowing that when you desire to be compassionate you also receive it.

You make the effort to bring forth compassion every day of your life because it feels good. You take a few deep breaths and center into your body. You bring to mind a person who makes you smile….someone who makes you very happy. You begin to imagine that person in front of you. You let yourself feel into being in that person's presence. You reflect and enjoy the beautiful moments shared together. You also recognize how vulnerable this person is because they experience sickness, aging and death. You too have the same vulnerabilities. You recognize this person wants to be happy and free from struggle. You realize this person also has the same wants. You see the same qualities in this person as you have in yourself. You feel compassion for this person as you feel for yourself.

How to Bring Gifts of Compassion in Your Life?

You understand people walk their own path, but their destination is the same. You realize we are all on the same journey in life. You cooperate with others so all can achieve the same goals of happiness, joy and freedom. Here are ways you can bring gifts of compassion:

a. **Bring Compassion to all of Your Life – Your Compassion is Your True Strength.** You bring compassion to all of life as it is your catalyst to power. You step into a powerful emotion within a realm between being you and your Higher Self. You feel compassion as the energy behind it creates a two-way interaction. You begin to feel an us rather than a feeling of separation. You develop compassion, and you feel it in your heart and soul. You feel compassion for yourself, another person, humanity, and Mother Earth.

b. **Love and Accept Yourself.** You are aware your experiences in life have a direct correlation to how much you love yourself. When you love yourself, you feel centered, loving and grounded. When you shift from loving yourself, you begin to feel frustrated, angry, sad…all fear-based emotions. Your inner work is a reflection of how much you truly love and accept yourself. You are aware of the many choices to love and acccpt yourself (for example a love relationship with another, comfort eating to fill a void, or volunteering or giving to others, etc.). You recognize nothing ever really comes and goes in life; it simply changes. You now love the beginnings and the endings…accepting what is. Life itself teaches you everything you need to know, so there is never a need to see outside of yourself for a solution because the answer is within.

You choose to love and accept yourself by going within…and you feel centered, loving and grounded when you do. You feel open to a truly loving Self who is open to ALL of life. You recognize to love and accept oneself takes practice…as it can be easy to shift back to an old pattern. Your awareness of the wisdom you already have within is what will help you shift back to your practice to love and accept yourself.

c. **Focus on Breathing Deeply. Breathe in. Breathe out. Scan Your Body. You're Here. You're Alive**.

You breathe deeply and slowly allowing your breath to form its own natural rhythm. You maintain your awareness of your breath as a way to alter your internal state and keep you present. With each deep breath, you calm your mind, slow your heart rate, lower your blood pressure and break free of life stressors.

You practice focusing on breathing deeply using simple steps. You sit up straight, focus on the area just below your navel, inhale through your nose with your mouth closed, exhale through your mouth keeping your lips gently pressed together. You inhale for two seconds, exhale for four seconds. Place your right hand over your belly and let the air fill you up, and then let the air out like a balloon. You feel how your belly rises as you breathe in and falls as you breathe out.

You scan your body to get in touch with any information that your body may be storing. Ask yourself, "What do I feel in this moment? Do I feel any tension or lightness?" You regularly scan your body for tension and place your attention on that part of your body to mindfully encourage it to relax.

d. **Know You Have the Freedom to Make Choices and Respond With a Higher Thought in Mind.** You are aware you are an expression of your thoughts. Before any action, you wait for the space in between your thoughts before responding. You inherently understand your conscious thoughts are a form of energy that always stays within your being. You witness your thoughts so you may choose to become more of what you want to be. You are creating patterns of thought both consciously and unconsciously. You take what life gives you and handle it as best as you can by responding with a Higher thought in mind.

e. **Invoke Your Senses to Perceive and Feel It…Fully Experience It.** As you invoke touch, smell, taste, sight and hearing, each uniquely affects how you respond or react to life as well as how you perceive what is going on. You fully feel all of the emotions that are elicited and experience life fully.

f. **Connect With People Who Love You and Love You in Return.** You feel deeply connected to people who love you. You are fully seen and appreciated and secure in your relationships. You are open to receive love in return. You understand the importance of giving and receiving love. You initiate conversations and fully listen to what the other has to say. You give the gift of your presence to others, and they reciprocate. You value yourself and the people in your life.

Chapter 5: Truthfulness

To create heaven, you MUST be honest with yourself and others. Mask NO secrets and share your truth with complete compassion, limitless love, and undeniable understanding.

"Understanding comes with compassion and compassion comes with truthfulness."

~Amit Abraham

You find your truth in stillness. You then live your truth by living what you value. You love what you are doing. When you are living your truth your desires are met with a world of possibilities. You commit to doing your best while living your truth. You have the courage to bring awareness to the real you behind your filters. Living your truth allows you to drop your efforts to protect and disguise parts of yourself. You understand this is a process and are compassionate with yourself. You begin to question what is true. Your questions bring forth clarity of your personal truth and empower you to make choices aligned with your integrity. As you become self-aware you let go of the stories you tell yourself so you can create what you desire in life. You accept who you are in this moment. You understand living your truth is not about changing you…instead you become free and confident as you step into your own power. When you are living your truth you are resilient with all of life's changes no matter the outcome. Living your truth means your relationships with others are based on mutual respect. So you no longer find it necessary to create those white lies. You accept what is right for you and no longer need approval from others.

You recognize your self-awareness and introspection is the start of your self-improvement. You pay attention to your emotions and how they work as they help you understand why you do the things you do. Your self-awareness helps you to uncover your beliefs. Your awareness helps you explore areas of your life where you may be running on 'auto-pilot'. You recognize these areas are often when your conditioned patterns of thought and behavior arise. You understand you likely did not consciously choose your beliefs as they are often handed down by those close to you while growing up. Then later in life your beliefs gained strength and became strong beliefs. You recognize there is a possibility these beliefs are no longer true for you. You identify your beliefs that are no longer true and simply stop believing them.

You let your pain and struggle be your teachers. You

learn to listen to yourself and trust what you find deep inside. You live authentically as it is your pathway to happiness. You are comfortable with being who you are to yourself and others.

How to Bring Gifts of Truthfulness in Your Life?

You accept and take great care to recognize your own feelings. You do your best to look at yourself objectively. You witness your thoughts and shift when necessary to a Higher thought. You observe your behavior knowing there are consequences to all of what you do in your life. Here is how to bring gifts of truthfulness in your life:

a. **You Recognize Your Feelings.** You tune into your body. You ask yourself, "Where do I feel this emotion in my body? What does it feel like? What are my thoughts?" Your thoughts are what your mind says is your truth. You change "I am" thoughts to "I feel" thoughts. You know your thoughts are not your feelings…they do not depict how you feel. They depict what you think you feel, your false "truth." Your knowing creates space so you can go deeper to what is behind why you feel this way. You bring awareness to how you really feel.

b. **You Accept Feelings Without Judgement and Simply Feel Them.** You sit with the feeling that arises…leaving your thoughts aside from evidence gathering. You simply feel. Breathe in. Breathe out. You let your feeling flow until it is released.

c. **You Replace Old Beliefs That No Longer Serve You With New Beliefs Backed by Reasons.** You trust this new belief is your real truth. You repeat your new truth and witness your feelings that arise noticing how it feels compared to your old truth.

d. **You Do Something Positive With Your New Truth.** You express how you feel in that moment through some physical act such as writing, art, making music, dance, etc. Your physical action sets your new truth in your body; as you are aware, your body contains memories that you are not consciously aware of.

Chapter 6: Personal Development

Arriving at this point in your journey isn't by luck, nor is it by chance; your inquisitive and curious nature to positivity in life has got you here.

"The only impossible journey is the one you never begin."

~Anthony Robbins

You keep an open and active mind by trying to continuously learn something new to improve yourself. You create a simple life so you can devote more time and resources to personal development.

How to Bring Gifts of Personal Development in Your Life?

Your curiosity and passion brings personal development into your life. You invest in yourself so you can take inspired actions effectively, no matter what life delivers on your path. You set goals and create action steps to achieve them.

a. **Know That Every Day Teaches You Something That Can Help You on Your**

Path. You are aware that if you want something, there are unseen energies that work to make it happen. Each day teaches you that you are here for a purpose. You understand that life teaches you to take risks and make your dreams possible.

b. **Be Self-Aware and Open…There's Something to Learn About Who You Are, What You Want and What You Need.** You are open to developing a sense of who you are in this moment. You are aware of who you are as a whole person. You know your values. You are aware of your strengths, weaknesses, and habits…you continually assess as everything in life changes. You take inspired actions to learn who you are, what you want out of life and what you believe in.

c. **Meditate Daily. It Brings Wisdom in Your Life…A Knowingness of What Moves You Forward and What Holds You Back.** You are aware meditation helps you reconnect and find a deeper sense of joy. You understand meditation calms the chatter in your mind, brings awareness and presence. When you meditate, be aware of a response feeling…it floods you with a tingling sensation or touches you on your head.

Chapter 7: Authentic Love

*You're devoted to authentic love —
through compassion, patience, kindness
and determination to understand
everyone who needs your help, advice or
simply lend your ear.*

"Real authentic love is something that begins with you loving yourself."

~Dr. D Ivan Young

You recognize authentic love has no endings as it simply keeps expanding. It is unconditional and available to all. You understand that if you truly love one thing but hate another, you are expressing conditional love. You grasp that to express authentic love, it has to be for all. If you simply take away all the labels we have for each other, you come to an understanding each of us matters...labels are the parts of us that are not important. We are all part of each other.

How to Bring Gifts of Authentic Love in Your Life?

You align with your values and purpose by being committed to living and loving. You express gratitude. You appreciate all that you do and all that you are.

a. **Be Still and Ground Yourself…Be Calm.** You acknowledge that you are authentic love. You take deep, full breaths all the way down to your belly. You breathe in through your nose and you exhale through your mouth (exhaling longer than inhaling). You imagine your feet have roots like a tree and are grounded deep into Mother Earth. You feel her energy flowing through you. Be still. Be Calm. Love flows through you…you are love.

b. **Connect to a Higher Vision of Life Because Everything You Pay Attention to From That View Expands in Awareness.** You connect to a Higher vision of life by taking your consciousness beyond just you. You understand whatever you pay attention to expands in awareness. You see what you bring closer to yourself as you connect within. When you connect to a Higher vision of life you open your mind and heart to seek knowledge and wisdom. You open your heart with love. You are always aware of your inner world as it is tuned in to the purpose of your life.

Your intention is the pathway to connect to your Higher Self.

c. **Cherish All of Life—The Good and The Bad…It's Part of a Divine Plan for You to Learn and Grow.** You look at your life experience and do your best to see the gifts in all of it. You surrender to life as it offers you infinite freedom and possibilities. You can let go of the struggle and choose a different feeling. You accept life on life's terms as you understand that at the level of Spirit everything is unfolding perfectly. You believe every life has value and hope. You see yourself and others in the light fully capable of escaping the painful illusions of the dark. You understand that a paradox of being spiritual is that good and bad exist at the same time. You embrace the mystery of life for there is always a divine plan for you to experience, learn and grow from.

Chapter 8: Inspiration

It doesn't matter who you are, or what life's thrown at you...trauma will ALWAYS pass. You inspire others to never give up hope and tirelessly reassure them that they'll find perfect harmony within themselves.

"Never give up on what you really want to do. The person with big dreams is more powerful than one with all the facts."

~Albert Einstein

You are an amazing and courageous person. From the realm of your desire, you are reclaiming your own personal power from the effects of trauma. You've found a deep and profound connection in someone or something greater than yourself to support you in your healing process. You feel in your heart you have something to share to help others. The beginning of your healing and transformation has become possible because you are giving yourself the time to change your perspective from within. You see that it is possible to rewrite the story of your past so that pain becomes meaningful and actually encourages your growth and transformation. You are not only inspiring yourself with your shift in feelings, you now see the possibility of sharing your transformation to help others heal.

You are curious and hopeful about life. You know what you want. You commit to doing what you are passionate about and the Universe will act accordingly. You focus on what you are feeling. You feel moved to create love, joy, passion and purpose in your life. You feel joy and happiness a whole lot more. You do what you are passionate about.

You continue to stay connected as you've also found inspiration in nature. You take walks in nature. You walk on a beach. You lie down on Mother Earth and feel her support you. You relax and then move on to the next best feeling. You feel all of life around you…welcome home!

How to Bring Gifts of Inspiration in Your Life?

You are curious and hopeful about life. You are re-visioning your life. You ask yourself, "Is this true for me?" And if the response comes from your heart and your Higher thought…you know what you want. You commit to doing what you are passionate about, and the Universe acts accordingly. You focus on what you are feeling. You feel moved to create love, joy, passion, and purpose in your life. You are opening to the possibility of sharing your healing process and transformation with others. You feel joy and happiness a whole lot more. You do what you are passionate about.

a. **You Have the Courage to Bring Your Gifts to Light.** You persevere with great courage and conviction and do not rest until your dreams are fulfilled. Your positive thoughts help you develop the physical and mental courage to act with conviction.

b. **You are Unique and Amazing. Your Resolve, Faith, and Spirit Encourages Healing.**

"Faith is seeing light with your heart when all your eyes see is darkness."

~anonymous

You are awesome! People see you for what you really are. You are great! You are unique and amazing! There is no one like you. You've been through it. You know. You have so much life experiences to share and look forward to helping others who struggle. You are a blessing to everyone!

c. **You Act in the Spirit of Love Based on What You Thus Learned.** You've listened to the deeper voice within you and now take inspired actions based on your core values to navigate life. You are love…and that expands in ways you never imagined. You feel it. It is the clearest and most vivid picture of what you learned about thus far…your connection with your Source. You are a source of light and strength for yourself and others.

d. **You Have Passion and Purpose in All You Do, With All Your Heart.** You are open to the infinite possibilities in life. With your values as your foundation, you step into your own destiny. You embrace, with all of your heart, your true purpose in life.

e. **You Live More Calmly, Courageously and Enthusiastically, With Positive Results That Surprise You.** You recognize your purpose resides within…you sit in complete silence and listen for messages from your heart. You courageously embrace change. You heal anything that may hold you back. You enthusiastically take inspired actions to all that you want in life acting as if it already manifested…and to your delight, the Universe delivers.

"The right path to live on is to live with the right values and right universal character and to be an instrument of the grace within us all."

~Radhanath Swami

Chapter 9: Putting It All Together

Be yourself. You are the creator of your own reality.

"Never change who you are so that other people will like you. Just be yourself and the right people will love you just for being you."

~Unknown

You are whole. You are being true to yourself. You are perfection in the light and your thoughts reflect your light.

No matter what values you choose, it is simply an expression of yourself. You believe in yourself. You have the impetus to take inspired actions to move toward your intention. You are aware of how you want to experience life and successfully manifest your desires. You manifest what you desire by matching it to your basic beliefs and values about yourself. You are free to manifest your unique talents and abilities. You honor your uniqueness by opening up to that which you desire. You honor your own values, beliefs, abilities by manifesting your own reality. As opportunities open, your experience is a fulfilling creation. You traverse an infinite number of opportunities. You express from your own heart. You are a manifestation of the divine. Your uniqueness sets you apart from others.

You know what you want. You know what you desire. You desire what you believe. Your belief is your desire becoming...and you feel good. You understand that the thought of desire is supported by the whole of you. You are aware that if you challenge the truth, there is resistance within you. You realize that the thought of wanted and unwanted at the same time causes resistance within you.

You avoid coming to a conclusion that a desire is not because it is not yet or seen completely by you. You recognize what you want is already here and it does not have to be seen, heard, tasted, smelled or touched. You hold the true vibrational version of who you are rather than let what has already manifested be the truth that you decide. This is the part of you allowing for your connection to Source.

You use the power of your focus and thoughts to create what it is you want in life. You came here to experience, to create, and to love. You find pleasure and joy in using your thoughts, your mind, your perspective in order to create around you what it is that you choose...not what someone has chosen for you. You allow your own blessings because you are

Chapter 9: Putting It All Together

Be yourself. You are the creator of your own reality.

"Never change who you are so that other people will like you. Just be yourself and the right people will love you just for being you."

~Unknown

You are whole. You are being true to yourself. You are perfection in the light and your thoughts reflect your light.

No matter what values you choose, it is simply an expression of yourself. You believe in yourself. You have the impetus to take inspired actions to move toward your intention. You are aware of how you want to experience life and successfully manifest your desires. You manifest what you desire by matching it to your basic beliefs and values about yourself. You are free to manifest your unique talents and abilities. You honor your uniqueness by opening up to that which you desire. You honor your own values, beliefs, abilities by manifesting your own reality. As opportunities open, your experience is a fulfilling creation. You traverse an infinite number of opportunities. You express from your own heart. You are a manifestation of the divine. Your uniqueness sets you apart from others.

You know what you want. You know what you desire. You desire what you believe. Your belief is your desire becoming...and you feel good. You understand that the thought of desire is supported by the whole of you. You are aware that if you challenge the truth, there is resistance within you. You realize that the thought of wanted and unwanted at the same time causes resistance within you.

You avoid coming to a conclusion that a desire is not because it is not yet or seen completely by you. You recognize what you want is already here and it does not have to be seen, heard, tasted, smelled or touched. You hold the true vibrational version of who you are rather than let what has already manifested be the truth that you decide. This is the part of you allowing for your connection to Source.

You use the power of your focus and thoughts to create what it is you want in life. You came here to experience, to create, and to love. You find pleasure and joy in using your thoughts, your mind, your perspective in order to create around you what it is that you choose...not what someone has chosen for you. You allow your own blessings because you are blessed… you are worthy. You create your own world. You are a vibrational being who creates through the power of your thought. Your thoughts matter over everything in life.

You cannot look at the 'what is' if the 'what is' is lacking something you want. Manifesting what you want is all about focusing and your thoughts. You are aware that if you look around and you do not have what you want, it means your thoughts are not working for you. You pay attention to the way you feel…because the subject of your thought is not as important as to the way it feels.

For your expansion…for your enlightenment…you matter a lot. You claim your spot in life because you are here purposefully…you matter to all that is. You matter to you. Your thoughts are what your inner being is thinking right now. You are aware Source is always flowing to you. Source knows who you are right now. Source knows your desires and worthiness. Source always knows your value, and when you devalue yourself or someone else, your vibration won't match with Source. You create your own reality, and you do it by your focus, and you can tell by the way you feel how you are doing. You care about how you feel and you shift your thoughts by trying to feel better and better. It is your Higher thought that is the evidence you need to demonstrate that what you want has already manifested.

Chapter 10: Your Next Steps?

Define your values and set your goals.

"Wisdom is knowing what to do next; virtue is doing it."

~David Starr Jordan

You choose values that resonate with you most in your life now. Not sure? You use prayer to ask God. You meditate to listen to your God. Through a feeling sense you create what you desire to experience through focused creation.

You desire change in your life. You desire to live your truth and live mindfully. As you change your expression you change your part of the greater whole. You have the courage to live a life you truly want and not defined by what others expect of you. You now determine what your deepest values are and what is meaningful to you.

How To Go Within To Choose Your Values?

Your values are always within. You are aware there is no work necessary as your divine voice will help you chose values that are aligned with your true purpose. Follow these six steps to help you choose your values:

1) **Reflect a Moment When You Felt Happy and Fulfilled**

    You recall a moment when you felt happy and fulfilled…when you felt totally yourself. You take your time. When you are ready you take notes about that moment and write it in your journal or type it in your computer. You simply describe that moment in a paragraph or two.

2) **Identify Values Being Expressed in That Moment**

    As you consider what values were being expressed in that happy moment, identify them, then list them in your journal or computer.

3) **Choose Your Most Important Values**

    From the list of values, ask yourself, "Does it hold true for me today? Which value is most important to me in my life?" Choose a close second value. Choose one or two values that hold true for you today.

4) Write What Your Values Mean to You in YOUR Life

For each chosen value write a few sentences about what it means to you in your life.

5) Choose Values That <u>Feel</u> Right for YOU

Define what each value you chose means to you. Everyone has an individual expression of what a value means to them.

6) Repeat the First Five Steps Until You Have 5 to 7 Values for Yourself.

You now know your values and have a deep sense of your direction life. You recognize your values can change anytime you desire. You are aware your values are your foundation of what exists in the present moment. You values can be drawn on anytime that you choose.

You Now Know Your Values…What Next?

Your values are a part of your navigation system for life. You are aware values are in the present moment. You now have the foundation to start to set your life goals. You ask yourself, "What is it I want in life?

What is it that I desire to manifest? What do I need do to make my dreams come true?" You reflect on your biggest desires. You even create a list by jotting them down on a piece of paper. You take some time to reflect on your goals and then choose the one that is your biggest, most ambitious goal. Now you imagine what it would be like if you realized that goal in every way you dreamed it could be. You imagine how you would really feel achieving this goal. Take your time and list words that describe how you feel with your dreams coming true. Your description begins to bring your goal into focus. You feel joy and happiness as your imagined goal gets realized. Your present moment feelings help you focus on experiencing what it is you truly want in life.

You have chosen your biggest, most ambitious goal and now you are ready to set inspired actions to achieve it. Does inspired actions sound familiar? You can refer to Chapter 3 on authenticity to refresh yourself on how to set inspired actions. Always remember you have everything you need within.

You've identified your values to begin to create the life you want today. As you explored your values, you too can see gifts within those values. Your values guide and shape your priorities and responses to life experiences. Your inspired actions and thoughts are aligned with your values…and you are experiencing a whole lot of happiness and joy.

You can create the life you want. You can create anything you desire. You can create heaven wherever you are (the "I AM")…and the 'I Am' is the healing power within you. You can create a new dream. There is no limit on your power to heal and transform every aspect of your life. Because of your awareness, you are the creator of the heaven you choose to live in life, no matter where you are in life.

ABOUT THE AUTHOR

Janine Naus is a author, speaker and transformational life coach. She is passionately committed to guiding struggling women who are ready to heal feelings of powerlessness and frustration due to trauma, WHO WANT to REMOVE THEIR FEARS ONCE AND FOR ALL and WANT TO LEAVE all the sadness behind and enjoy increased serenity and calmness. She helps women open their heart to love themselves again and trust love from others…to move forward with a positive attitude. When she is not working with her amazing clients, she is enjoying walking the boardwalk along the shores of the Chesapeake Bay in Chesapeake Beach, MD with her dog Frankie.

Visit her and more at: www.janinenaus.com.

Get your free work-thru booklet called *"Discovering Secrets To Your True Nature And Inspired Actions From Your Heart Not Your Hurt"* on the author's website.

www.ingramcontent.com/pod-product-compliance
Lightning Source LLC
Chambersburg PA
CBHW020020050426
42450CB00005B/573